LET'S GO 6

4th Edition

STUDENT BOOK

Ritsuko Nakata

Karen Frazier

Barbara Hoskins

songs and chants by Carolyn Graham

OXFORD

UNIVERSITY PRESS

OXFORD
UNIVERSITY PRESS

198 Madison Avenue
New York, NY 10016 USA

Great Clarendon Street, Oxford, OX2 6DP, United Kingdom

Oxford University Press is a department of the University of Oxford.
It furthers the University's objective of excellence in research, scholarship,
and education by publishing worldwide. Oxford is a registered trade
mark of Oxford University Press in the UK and in certain other countries

General Manager, American ELT: Laura Pearson
Executive Publishing Manager: Shelagh Speers
Senior Managing Editor: Anne Stribling
Project Editor: June Schwartz
Art, Design, and Production Director: Susan Sanguily
Design Manager: Lisa Donovan
Designer: Sangeeta E. Ramcharan
Electronic Production Manager: Julie Armstrong
Production Artist: Elissa Santos
Image Manager: Trisha Masterson
Image Editor: Joe Kassner
Production Coordinator: Christopher Espejo
Senior Manufacturing Controller: Eve Wong

ISBN: 978 0 19 464149 4

Printed in China

This book is printed on paper from certified and well-managed sources

ACKNOWLEDGEMENTS
*The authors and publisher are grateful to those who have given permission to reproduce
the following extracts and adaptations of copyright material:*

Illustrations by: Bernard Adnet: 9(t), 63; Ilias Arahovitis: 24 (t), 25(b), 31(t), 35(b),
37(t), 41(b), 44(t); Bob Berry: 5(b), 20; Scott Burroughs: 38(t), 52(t); Terri Chicko
/ Jesse Graber: 13, 29, 69; Bob Depew: 40, 42(b), 48, 50(b), 52(b), 58, 60(b), 62(b),
66, 68(b); James Elston: 32(t), 33, 35(t), 38(b); Kathi Ember: 6(t), 42(t), 43(t); Roc
Goudreau: 45; Daniel Griffo: 2, 3, and cats on pages 4, 6, 8, 10, 12, 14, 16, 18,
22, 24, 26, 28, 30, 32, 34, 36, 40, 42, 44, 46, 48, 50, 52, 54, 58, 60, 62, 64, 66, 68,
70, and 72; Diane Hays: 31(b); John Hom: 4, 5(t), 6(b), 8(b), 12, 14(b), 16(b), 22,
24 (b), 26(b), 30, 32(b), 34(b), 44(b); Darryl Ligasan: 10, 11, 26(t), 47, 64, 65, 74;
David Lowe: 18, 19, 60(t); Colleen Madden: 34(t), 49(t), 61(b), 62(t); Katie McDee:
27; Karen Minot: 39; Sherry Rogers: 25(t), 51, 55, 59(b), 61(t), 73; Christine
Schneider: 70, 71; Janet Skiles: 49(b), 57; Sam Tomasello: 16(t), 67; Chris Vallo:
7, 8(t), 9(b), 17, 41(t), 50(t), 56, 68(t); Christina Wald: 14(t), 15, 37(b); Penny
Weber: 23, 43(b), 53, 59(t).

*The publishers would like to thank the following for their kind permission to reproduce
photographs:* pg. 10 Ocean/Corbis (children); pg. 10-11 Corbis Flirt/Alamy
(popsicles); pg. 11 mikeledray/shutterstock.com (popsicle); pg. 18 Darrin
Henry/shutterstock.com (boy); pg. 18-19 Jenny Horne/istockphoto.com (beach
bkgd); pg. 19 Nick M. Do/istockphoto.com (starfish); pg. 21 Jessica Peterson/
Rubberball/Corbis (children); pg. 21 Dan Breckwoldt/shutterstock.com (Egypt);
pg. 21 Travelpix/Alamy (Mexico); pg. 21 JTB Photo Communications, Inc./
Alamy (Japan); pg. 28 Rob Marmion/shutterstock.com (boy with sign); pg. 28
Robert Cable/Getty Images (trash); pg. 28 Leland Bobbe/Photodisc/Getty Images
(children with garbage bags); pg. 28 Jason Patrick Ross/shutterstock.com
(butterfly); pg. 28 Image Source/Getty Images (bench); pg. 28-29 Akira Kaede/
Getty Images (garden bkgd); pg. 29 DNY59/istockphoto.com (tree); pg. 36
kk-artworks/shutterstock.com (Earth); pg. 36 Eduardo Rivero/shutterstock.com
(toucan); pg. 36 NOAA/SCIENCE PHOTO LIBRARY (star bkgd); pg. 36-37 Hayri
Er/istockphoto.com (star bkgd); pg. 37 GYRO PHOTOGRAPHY/amanaimagesRF/
Getty Images (Earth); pg. 39 Jessica Peterson/Rubberball/Corbis (children);
pg. 39 gary yim/shutterstock.com (statues with clouds); pg. 39 Kachalkina
Veronika/shutterstock.com (statues with woods); pg. 46 Prisma Bildagentur
AG/Alamy (plantation); pg. 46 foodfolio/Alamy (cake); pg. 46 Jose Luis Pelaez
Inc/Blend Images/Getty Images (hot cocoa); pg. 46 Mauritius/SuperStock (cacao
seeds); pg. 46-47 Jupiterimages/Comstock Images/Getty Images (chocolate
shavings); pg. 47 Chris Ted/Digital Vision/Getty Images (stacked chocolate);
pg. 54 Hans Neleman/The Image Bank/Getty Images (girl in yellow, couple
balancing); pg. 54 Frans Lemmens/The Image Bank/Getty Images (bicycles);
pg. 54-55 Danish Khan/istockphoto.com (canopy); pg. 55 Ljupco/istockphoto.
com (balloons); pg. 57 Jessica Peterson/Rubberball/Corbis (children); pg. 57
Phecsone/shutterstock.com (paper); pg. 57 Petr Svarc/Alamy (Egypt); pg. 57
David Ball/Alamy (Rosetta Stone); pg. 57 Steven Dusk/Alamy (Hieroglyphics);
pg. 64 Nathan Blaney/iStock Exclusive/Getty Images (girl); pg. 64-65 sonyae/
istockphoto.com (curtain); pg. 72 Dr. Ronald H. Cohn/The Gorilla Foundation/
koko.org (Koko, All); pg. 72-73 Jon Schulte/istockphoto.com (tablecloth bkgd);
pg. 73 Michelle Gibson/istockphoto.com (cupcake); pg. 75 Jessica Peterson/
Rubberball/Corbis (children); pg. 75 Edyta Pawlowska/shutterstock.com
(Aerial); pg. 75 GlowImages/Alamy (Condor, Spider).

Text Design: Molly K. Scanlon
Cover Design: Susan Sanguily
Cover Illustrator: Daniel Griffo

Table of Contents

Kate

Andy

Jenny

Scott

Let's Talk

Let's Learn

Let's Learn More

Let's Read

Let's Review

Let's Remember

Let's Talk

A Listen and say. CD1 03

Kate: Whose scarf is that?

Jenny: It's Anna's scarf.

Kate: Whose mittens are those?

Jenny: They're hers, too.

Kate: Is that her glove, too?

Jenny: No, it isn't. I think it's Jim's glove.

Kate: Which boy is Jim?

Jenny: He's the boy over there.

Jenny: Jim, I think this is yours.

Jim: Oh! Thanks for finding it.

Jenny: You're welcome.

CD1 04

Thanks for finding it.
You're welcome.

1. scarf

2. mittens

3. gloves

4. glasses

5. belt

6. watch

Kate

Andy

Jenny

Scott

Anna

Jim

CD1 06

Whose scarf is that?
It's Anna's scarf.
It's hers.

my scarf = mine
her scarf = hers
his scarf = his
your scarf = yours

C Listen and sing. CD1 07

Whose Boots Are These?

Whose boots are these?
Whose boots are these?
Whose boots are these?
  They're mine. They're my boots.

Whose boots are those?
Whose boots are those?
Whose boots are those?
  They're mine. They're my boots.

Whose boots are these?
Whose boots are these?
Whose boots are these?
  They're mine.

Are you sure they're yours?
All of them?
  Yes, I'm sure they're mine.

Unit 1 School Days **5**

Let's Learn

A Learn the words.

1. watering the plants

2. feeding the fish

3. writing on the board

4. talking to the teacher

5. reading a textbook

6. writing an essay

B Ask and answer.

There is a new teacher in the class. She is learning the names of her students.

Which boy is Scott?
He's the boy who is watering the plants.

C Ask and answer. (CD1 10)

Lisa

Kevin

Luke

TODAY

Abby

1

2

3

4

Which girl is Lisa?
She's the girl who is writing an essay.

D Listen and chant. (CD1 11) ♪♫

Kim's Father Was Born in Seoul

Kim's father was born in Seoul.
They speak Korean at home.
 Which man is Kim's father?
He's the man who's waiting
 for the phone.

Ann's sister was born in Rome.
They speak Italian at home.
 Which girl is Ann's sister?
She's the girl who's standing
 by the phone.

Ken's brother was born in Japan.
They speak Japanese at home.
 Which boy is Ken's brother?
He's the boy who's talking
 on the phone.

Let's Learn More

A Learn the words. CD1 12

1. talking on his cell phone

2. reading a magazine

3. walking in the park

4. drinking some water

5. playing a game

6. sitting on a bench

B Make sentences. CD1 13

Jenny was sitting on a bench when it started to rain.
What were Andy, Kate, and Scott doing?

Jenny **was** sitting on a bench **when** it started to rain.

C Play a game. Ask and answer.

> What was she doing when it started to rain?
> She was skateboarding when it started to rain.

START

END

D Ask your partner.

1.

What was she doing when she heard the noise?

2.

What was he doing when he saw the skunk?

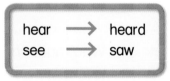

| hear | → | heard |
| see | → | saw |

A Listen and read along. Then read again. (CD1 16)

THE FIRST ICE POP

Do you like ice pops? A young boy made the first ice pop in 1905.

One cold night, Frank was making soda water outside. He mixed soda powder and water in a cup. He was mixing the soda with a straw when he heard his mother. "Come inside, Frank," she said.

Frank forgot to take his cup with him. In the morning, he saw the cup. The soda water was frozen. He pulled the frozen soda out of the cup.

It was an ice pop!

New Words

ice pop
soda
mix
soda powder
straw
freeze → frozen

B Choose the correct answer. (CD1 17)

1. Who made the first ice pop?   ☐ Frank   ☐ Frank's mother

2. When did Frank make the ice pop?   ☐ in 1905   ☐ outside

C Understand the vocabulary.

> The soda water was frozen.

What does frozen mean?

a.

b.

c.

D Ask your partner.

1. Have you ever made an ice pop? What flavor was it?
2. Why did the soda water freeze?

E Listen and write. Do you hear aw or ow? (CD1 18)

1. c_____ 2. s_____ 3. p_____der 4. str_____

F Learn about words. Read and write.

> I mix soda water every day.
> I mixed soda water yesterday.
> mix + ed = mixed

1. pull + ed = _____ 2. paint + ed = _____
3. play + ed = _____ 4. talk + ed = _____

A **Listen and say.** CD1 19

Scott: What a great day!
Kate: It sure was! But I'm tired now.
Scott: Me, too. We really walked a lot.

Kate: What did you like best?
Scott: I think I liked the penguins best.
Kate: They were cute.
Scott: What about you?

Kate: I liked the sharks.
Scott: They were scary!

CD1 20

What a great day!
It sure was!

B Say these.
CD1 21

1. She was amazed.
   The penguins were amazing.

2. He was bored.
   The movie was boring.

3. She was interested.
   The book was interesting.

4. He was tired.
   The race was tiring.

5. He was excited.
   The ride was exciting.

6. She was scared.
   The shark was scary.

C Listen and chant.
CD1 22

The Racing Chant

Look at those kids!
Look at them run!
This is exciting!
This is fun!

I'm excited!
Look at them run!
This is exciting!
This is fun!

Let's Learn

A Learn the words. (CD1 23)

1. an aquarium

2. a tour

3. a lecture

4. an exhibit

5. a shark

6. an octopus

B Make sentences. (CD1 24)

Andy and Jenny had a great day at the aquarium. All the exhibits were exciting. What was scary? What was interesting? What was amazing? What was tiring?

The shark was scary.

scary   amazing
interesting   tiring

C Make sentences. CD1 25

1. exhibit / amazing / amazed

2. sharks / exciting / excited

3. lecture / boring / bored

4. aquarium / interesting / interested

> The exhibit was amazing. She was amazed.

D Listen and chant. CD1 26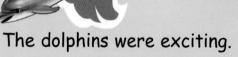

The Aquarium Chant

The aquarium was amazing.
I was amazed.
The sharks were really scary.
But they weren't scared.

The dolphins were exciting.
The kids were very excited.
But Grandma thought it was boring.
She was really bored.

Let's Learn More

A Learn the words. CD1 27

1. a jellyfish

2. a sea turtle

3. a squid

4. a video

5. a ride

6. a pedal boat

B Make sentences. CD1 28

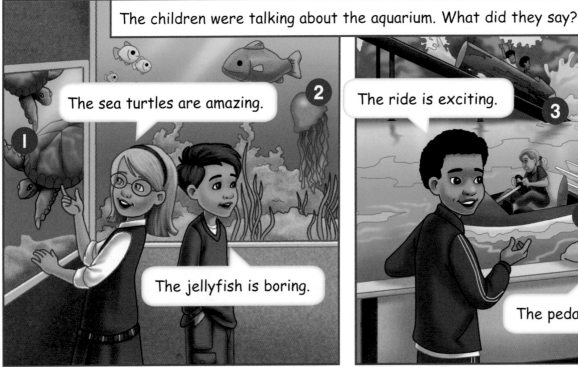

The children were talking about the aquarium. What did they say?

The sea turtles are amazing.

The jellyfish is boring.

The ride is exciting.

The pedal boat is tiring.

Kate **said** the sea turtles **were** amazing.

is → was
are → were

C Play a game. What did they say? (CD1 29)

He said he was amazed. She said the squid was scary.

Start

I'm amazed.

The squid is scary.

She is excited.

The lecture is boring.

He is scared.

They're tired.

End

The pedal boat is tiring.

The sea turtles are amazing.

The video is interesting.

The ride is exciting.

D What about you?

What do you think is exciting?
What do you think is boring?

Let's Read

A Listen and read along. Then read again. (CD1 30)

Waves in a Bottle

Do you like to look at waves when you go to the beach? You can look at waves in a bottle, too!

1. First, wash a bottle so you can reuse it. Put some water and a little blue color into the bottle.

water to here

2. Next, put oil into the bottle. You can put in some glitter, too.

3. Put some glue around the bottle cap and close the bottle. Close it tight!

When you move the bottle, you'll see waves!

New Words
waves
reuse
oil
glitter

B Choose the correct answer. (CD1 31)

1. What do you do first? ☐ wash the bottle ☐ close the bottle
2. What do you do last? ☐ wash the bottle ☐ close the bottle

C Understand the vocabulary.

First, wash the bottle so that you can reuse it.

What does reuse mean?

a.

b.

c.

D Ask your partner.

1. Do you like to go to the beach?
2. What do you like to do at the beach?

E Listen and write. Do you hear oi or oo?

CD1 32

1. c_____n   2. b_____k   3. _____l   4. c_____k   5. l_____k

F Learn about words. Read and write.

You can use a bottle.
Wash a bottle so that you can reuse it.

re + use = reuse

1. reread = re + _____
2. replay = re + _____
3. review = re + _____
4. remix = re + _____

Let's Review ✓

A Listen and check. (CD1 33)

1.

   A ☐   B ☐   C ☐

2.

   A ☐   B ☐   C ☐

3.

   A ☐   B ☐   C ☐

4.

   A ☐   B ☐   C ☐

B Listen and check. What did they say? (CD1 34)

1. **A** ☐ scared
   B ☐ scary

2. **A** ☐ exciting
   B ☐ excited

C Listen and check. (CD1 35)

1. It's interesting.   She's scared.

   A ☐   B ☐

2. He's tired.   It's boring.

   A ☐   B ☐

D Let's read about pyramids. (CD1 36)

Mystery Hunters

Matt and Megan's Blog

The Great Pyramids in Giza, Egypt

The Great Pyramid of Cholula, Mexico

Underwater Pyramids, Japan

Huge Ruins

There are many pyramids around the world. You can see pyramids in Egypt, in Africa, in Greece, in Mexico, and in China.

The most famous pyramids are in Egypt. The largest pyramid is in Mexico. But, the oldest pyramids may be underwater.

Divers have found ruins in the ocean near Japan. They think they have found a very old city. Some of the ruins look like pyramids.

Who built the underwater city?
Why did it sink?
Was there an earthquake?
Did the ocean rise?

It's a mystery.

New Words
famous
diver
ruins
sink
earthquake
rise
mystery

E Your turn!

Have you ever seen a pyramid?

Why do you think people built pyramids?

Why did the underwater pyramids sink?

What do you think? Write your opinion.

Let's Talk

A **Listen and say.** (CD1 37)

Kate: Hi, Andy. What are you doing here?
Andy: I need a present for my mother.
Kate: What are you going to get her?
Andy: I don't know.

Andy: What should I get her? Do you have any ideas?
Kate: Hmmm. You could get her a teapot. Or you could get her a cookbook.
Andy: She doesn't like tea, and she already has a lot of cookbooks.

Kate: How about a scarf?
Andy: That's a great idea! These scarves are beautiful!
Kate: I think you should get her this scarf.
Andy: Yes! She'll love it.

(CD1 38) How about a scarf? That's a great idea!

get = buy

B Say these. CD1 39

1. a scarf
2. a bracelet
3. a box of chocolates
4. a cookbook
5. a DVD
6. a book

C Look at B. Ask your partner.

1. mother
2. father
3. grandmother
4. grandfather

 CD1 40

What should she get her mother?

She should get | her / him | a bracelet.

D Listen and chant. CD1 41 ♪♫

I Need a Present for My Mother

I need a present for my mother.
What should I get her?
 How about a necklace?
She doesn't like jewelry.
 You could buy a nice T-shirt.
She doesn't wear T-shirts.
 You could give her a tennis racket.
She hates tennis.

You could make her a birthday cake.
I can't cook.
 You should take her out to dinner!
Great idea! She'll love it!

Let's Learn

A Learn the words. CD1 42

1. a video camera   2. a necklace   3. a ring   4. a novel

5. a stuffed toy   6. earrings   7. golf clubs   8. a model

B Ask and answer. CD1 43

The children are buying gifts for their families.
What should they get?

Should I get my sister a necklace or a ring?
You should get her a ring.

C Make sentences. (CD1 44)

They should get him a novel.

D Listen and chant. (CD1 45)

Today's My Brother's Birthday

Today's my brother's birthday.
What should I buy him?
What should I do?
What should I buy for my brother?
My older brother, Lou?

Buy him a jacket,
Buy him a coat,
Buy him a bicycle,
Buy him a boat.

Buy him an airplane,
Buy him a car,
Buy him a chocolate candy bar.

Let's Learn More

A Learn the words. CD1 46

1. bought a drink

2. made a bracelet

3. sent a picture

4. gave a present

5. showed a T-shirt

6. told a story

B Make sentences. CD1 47

Kate, Andy, and Jenny went to a fair. Jenny bought her brother a drink. Kate showed Andy a T-shirt. Andy sent Scott a picture.

soda $.75
ice cream $1
hot dogs $2.25
chips $.50

She showed him a T-shirt.

show	→	showed
send	→	sent
buy	→	bought

C Play a game. Ask and answer.

What did she make her?
She made her a bracelet.

buy	→	bought	give	→	gave
make	→	made	show	→	showed
send	→	sent	tell	→	told

D What about you?

Have you ever made something for your parents?
What did you make?

A Listen and read along. Then read again. (CD1 49)

HAPPINESS IS A CLEAN PARK

Before

My name is David and this was my park. I've lived next to this park since I was a baby. I liked the park, but there was a lot of trash. It was ugly.

Last autumn, my friends and I cleaned up the park. We put up posters and asked people to help us.

A lot of people came in the afternoon. Their kindness was amazing. We put the trash into bags and swept the sidewalks with brooms.

This is my park now. It's beautiful!

LET'S CLEAN UP OUR PARK

After

New Words	
happiness	sweep → swept
trash	sidewalks
autumn	brooms
kindness	

B Choose the correct answer. (CD1 50)

1. What did the park look like before they cleaned it up? ☐ beautiful ☐ ugly
2. What did the park look like after they cleaned it up? ☐ beautiful ☐ ugly

C Understand the vocabulary.

> I've lived next to this park since I was a baby.

What does since I was a baby mean?

a.  b.  c.

D Ask your partner.

1. Do you live near a park?
2. Have you ever cleaned up a park?

E Listen and write. Do you hear au or oo? (CD1 51)

1. br_____m   2. _____gust   3. aftern_____n   4. m_____n   5. _____tumn

F Learn about words. Read and write.

> They are kind.   kind + ness = kindness
> Their kindness is amazing.   happy − y + i = happiness

1. _____ + ness = sadness   2. _____ − y + i = happiness

3. _____ + ness = lightness   4. _____ − y + i = heaviness

A Listen and say. CD1 52

Kate: Where's the food court? Do you know?

Jenny: No, I don't. Let's look at the map.

Kate: Here it is. It's across from the music store.

Jenny: Where are we now?

Kate: We're here. We should go this way.

Jenny: There's the food court. Where are the boys?

Kate: They're over there, next to the ice cream shop.

Jenny: I see them!

CD1 53

Where are we now?
We're here.

B Practice the words. Ask and answer. CD1 54

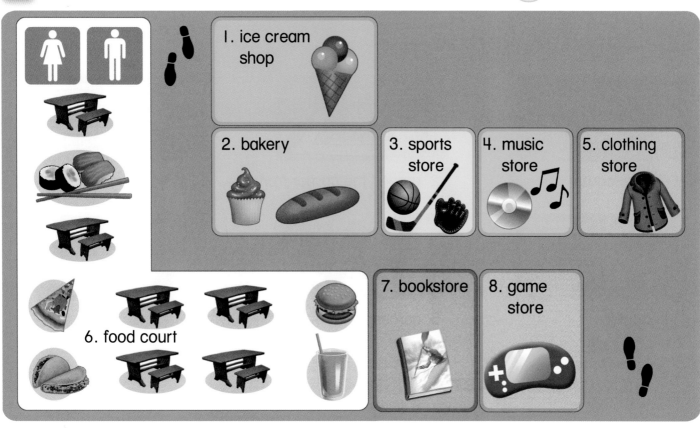

1. ice cream shop
2. bakery
3. sports store
4. music store
5. clothing store
6. food court
7. bookstore
8. game store

CD1 55

Where's the ice cream shop?
It's next to the bakery.

next to
across from
between

C Listen, point, and sing. CD1 56

Where's the Bookstore?

Where's the bookstore?
   It's next to the food court.
Where's the food court?
   It's across from the bakery.

Where's the bakery?
   It's next to the
   ice cream shop.
Come on! I'm hungry. Let's go!

Let's Learn

A Learn the words. CD1 57

1. on the corner

2. around the corner from

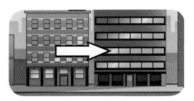

3. on the right

4. on the left

5. across the street from

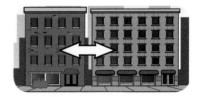

6. next to

B Ask and answer. CD1 58

Andy and Scott are looking for places in town.

Where's the ice cream shop?
It's on the corner. It's across the street from the bank.

C Make sentences. (CD1 59)

1. bakery

2. restaurant

3. music store

4. ice cream shop

5. bookstore

6. beauty shop

7. bank

8. grocery store

9. gift shop

10. library

The **bakery** **is** on the corner. **It's** next to the **restaurant**.

D What about you?

Where is the bank in your town?

Where is the library in your school?

Let's Learn More

A Learn the words. CD1 60

1. Go straight.

2. Go to the corner.

3. Turn left.

4. Turn right.

5. Go two blocks.

6. Cross the street.

B Ask and answer. CD1 61

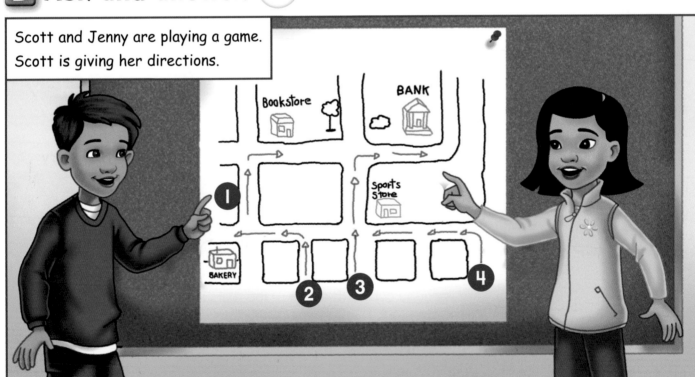

Scott and Jenny are playing a game.
Scott is giving her directions.

Go to the corner **and** turn right. **Where are you?**
I'm at the bookstore.

C Play a game.
Give directions. (CD1 62)

How do I get to the park?
Go two blocks **and** turn right.

× Start Here

DVD STORE · RESTAURANT · BAKERY · BOOKSTORE · PET STORE · BANK · AIRPORT

D Listen and chant. (CD1 63)

AUTO SHOW

I'm Looking for Joe

I'm looking for Joe. Where did he go?
  I think he went to the auto show.
How did he get there?
  I know.
  I saw him walk to the auto show.
  He walked two blocks and then turned right.
  He stopped for a minute at the traffic light.

  He crossed the street when the light turned green.
  Then he stopped on the corner to talk to Eileen.
  He said, "Eileen, come on, let's go."
  Then they went straight to the auto show.

A Listen and read along. Then read again. CD1 64

The Blue Planet

Earth is called the Blue Planet. Do you know why? The Earth looks blue from space because there is water on 70% of our planet.

Sometimes there are storms over warm ocean water. These are hurricanes. The wind is very strong, and it blows in a circle. North of the equator, hurricane winds blow counterclockwise. South of the equator, the winds blow clockwise.

Hurricanes form at the equator. It is very rainy and moist there. There are many different animals and beautiful plants.

New Words

planet
earth
space
hurricane
equator
counterclockwise
clockwise

B Choose the correct answer. CD1 65

1. Why is Earth called the Blue Planet?
   ☐ Because it's in space.
   ☐ Because there is water on 70% of the planet.

2. How do hurricane winds blow north of the equator?
   ☐ clockwise
   ☐ counterclockwise

C Understand the vocabulary.

> The winds blow clockwise.

What does clockwise mean?

a.

b.

c.

D Ask your partner.

1. Do you live north of the equator or south of the equator?
2. How will the hurricane winds blow here?

E Listen and write. Do you hear **ow** or **or**? (CD1 66)

1. bl_____   2. yell_____   3. st_____m   4. sn_____   5. n_____th

F Learn about words. Read and write.

> There is a lot of rain.
> It is very rainy.
>
> rain + y = rainy

1. _____ + _____ = windy

2. _____ + _____ = snowy

3. storm + _____ = _____

4. sleep + _____ = _____

A Listen and check. (CD1 67)

1.

A ☐   B ☐   C ☐

2.

A ☐   B ☐   C ☐

3.

A ☐   B ☐   C ☐

4.

A ☐   B ☐   C ☐

B Listen and check. (CD1 68)

1.

A ☐   B ☐

2.

A ☐   B ☐

C Listen and number. (CD1 69)

Mystery Hunters

Matt and Megan's **Blog**

Moai heads on Easter Island

More *moai* heads

Easter Island is located in the South Pacific Ocean

Easter Island: Mysterious Statues

Have you ever seen people moving a giant statue? They use a crane. How did ancient people move giant statues?

Ancient people on Easter Island carved more than 800 large stone statues, called *moai*. They put the *moai* around the island. Each *moai* is taller than an elephant and heavier than two elephants. How did people move them? There were no cranes a thousand years ago.

We can't ask the Easter Island people. They have disappeared. But we can still see their statues on the island.

It's a mystery.

New Words
giant
statue = moai
ancient
stone
a thousand
Easter Island
disappeared

E **Your turn!**

Have you ever seen people moving a statue?

How did the Easter Island people move the *moai*?

What do you think? Write your opinion.

A Listen and say. CD2 02

Kate: Have you met Anh? She's the girl who is talking to Jenny.

Scott: No, I haven't. Is she here on a homestay?

Kate: Yes, she is. She's staying with Jenny's family.

Scott: Really? Where's she from?

Kate: She's from Vietnam.

Scott: Does Anh speak English?

Kate: Yes, she does. She speaks Vietnamese and English, too.

Scott: I'd like to meet her.

Kate: OK, let's go. Excuse me, Jenny. Scott wants to meet Anh.

Scott: Hi, Anh! Are you enjoying your homestay?

Anh: Yes, I am. Have you ever been on a homestay?

Scott: Not yet, but I would like to go on one someday.

Anh: You should come to Vietnam and stay with my family.

Scott: That's a great idea. Thanks!

CD2 03

Have you met Anh?
Yes, I have.   No, I haven't.

B Practice the words. Ask and answer. (CD2 04)

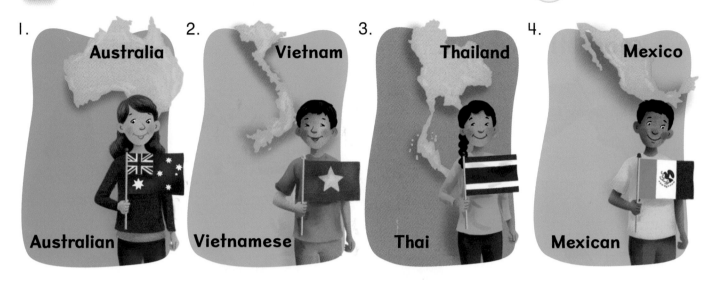

1. Australia — Australian
2. Vietnam — Vietnamese
3. Thailand — Thai
4. Mexico — Mexican

(CD2 05)

Where's she from?
She's from Australia. She's Australian.

C Listen and chant. (CD2 06)

Homestay Plans

I'm studying Spanish. How about you?
  I'm studying Spanish, too.
I want to go on a homestay.
  I want to do that, too.
When could we go on a homestay?
  We could leave at the end of May.
Where could we practice our Spanish?
  We could go to Monterrey.

He's studying English. How about Sue?
  She's studying English, too.
He wants to go on a homestay.
  She wants to do that, too.

Do you think they could go on a
  homestay?
  Yes, I think they could.
Where could they practice
  their English?
  They could go to Hollywood!

Let's Learn

A Learn the words. CD2 07

1. Brazil
2. Portuguese — Bom dia!
3. France
4. French — Bonjour!

5. Italy
6. Italian — Buongiorno!
7. Mexico
8. Spanish — ¡Buenos días!

B Make sentences. CD2 08

Jenny and Andy are learning about countries and languages.

People in Mexico speak Spanish.
Spanish is spoken in Mexico.

C Ask and answer. CD2 09

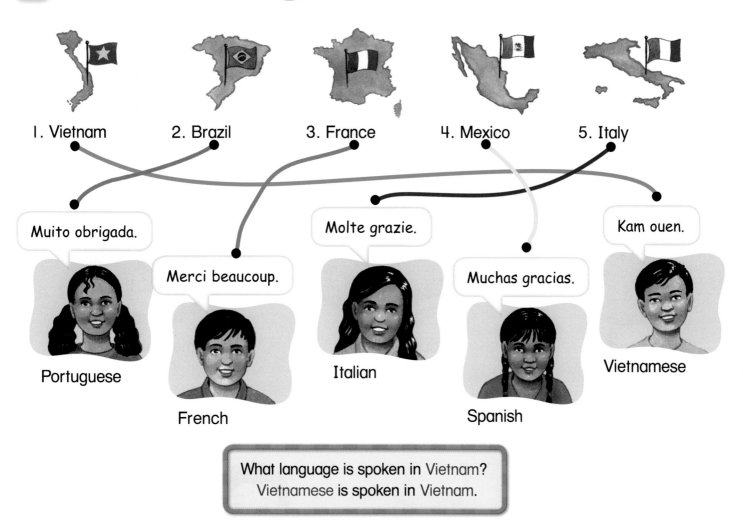

1. Vietnam
2. Brazil
3. France
4. Mexico
5. Italy

Muito obrigada.

Merci beaucoup.

Molte grazie.

Muchas gracias.

Kam ouen.

Portuguese

French

Italian

Spanish

Vietnamese

What language is spoken in Vietnam?
Vietnamese is spoken in Vietnam.

D Listen and sing. CD2 10

Have You Met Alice?

Bom dia!

Have you met Alice?
She was born in Dallas.
But now she goes to school in Brazil.
  Does she speak Portuguese?
Yes, she does.
English is not spoken at her school.

Have you met Maria?
She was born in Korea.
But her mother was born in Rome.
Her father's Korean.
Her mother's Italian.
And Korean is spoken at home.

Annyeong.

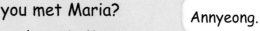

Let's Learn More

A Learn the words. (CD2 11)

1. black beans

2. croissants

3. spaghetti

4. rice noodles

5. burritos

6. meat pies

B Ask and answer. (CD2 12)

Kate and Jenny like eating foods from different countries.

Where are black beans eaten?
Black beans **are eaten** in Brazil.

Croissants **are eaten** in France.
Spanish **is spoken** in Mexico.

START

END

D **What about you?**

What languages are spoken in your classroom?
What foods are eaten in your country?

A Listen and read along. Then read again. (CD2 14)

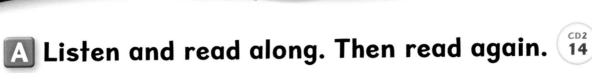

Chocolate

Do you like chocolate? It's in candy, cakes, and bread, and we have chocolate drinks, too. It's sweet and delicious!

We can thank the Mexicans. They discovered cacao seeds. They made a chocolate drink from the seeds, but it was very bitter.

Later, Spanish people came to Mexico. They put sugar in their chocolate. People liked the sweet chocolate. Only rich people drank chocolate because it was very expensive.

I love eating chocolate! I have a lot of chocolate in my house. I'm very happy. Thank you, Mexico!

New Words
discover
cacao seeds
Spanish people

B Choose the correct answer. (CD2 15)

1. How did the Mexican chocolate drink taste? ☐ sweet ☐ bitter
2. How did the Spanish chocolate drink taste? ☐ sweet ☐ bitter

C Understand the vocabulary.

They **discovered** cacao seeds.

What does **discover** mean?

a.

b.

c.

D Ask your partner.

1. Do you like chocolate?
2. Do you like sweet chocolate or bitter chocolate?

E Listen and write. Do you hear ea or ou? CD2 16

1. c_____nt 2. br_____d 3. h_____d 4. h_____se

F Learn about words. Read and write.

I eat chocolate.
I love eating chocolate.

eat + ing = eating

1. drink + ing = _____

2. discover + _____ = _____

3. _____ + _____ = singing

4. _____ + _____ = blowing

A **Listen and say.** CD2 17

Scott: I'm sorry I'm late.
Andy: That's OK.
Scott: How long have you been waiting?
Andy: Not long. Only a few minutes.

Scott: Have you already bought your ticket?
Andy: Yes, I have, and I bought your ticket, too!
Scott: Wow, thanks!

Scott: I'm excited to see this movie!
Andy: Me, too. I've heard it's funny.
Scott: Really? I've heard it's scary.
Andy: Oh. Maybe it's scary and funny.

CD2 18 | Have you already bought your ticket?
Yes, I have.   No, not yet.

I have = I've

B Practice the words. Make sentences. CD2 19

1. cleaned his desk

2. washed her hands

3. watched the movie

4. walked the dog

5. gone to the store

6. eaten dinner

7. fed the cat

8. done his homework

CD2 20

He **has already** cleaned his desk.
He **hasn't** cleaned his desk **yet**.

C Listen and chant. CD2 21

Have You Finished Your Homework?

Have you finished your homework?
  No, not yet.
You haven't finished?
  No, not yet.
  How about you?
I've already finished mine.
  Good for you!

Have you been to France?
  No, not yet.
You haven't been to France?
  No, not yet.

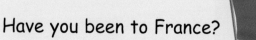

How about you?
I've already been there twice.
  Lucky you!

Have you eaten dinner?
  No, not yet.
You haven't eaten dinner?
  No, not yet.
  How about you?
I haven't eaten lunch or dinner.
  Poor you!

Unit 6 Doing Things **49**

Let's Learn

A Learn the words. CD2 22

1. studied English

2. lived in New York

3. taught French

4. played soccer

5. had a cat

6. been at the hotel

B Ask and answer. CD2 23

Jenny is interviewing her French teacher.

	for	since
1	five years	2007
2	one year	last year
3	three months	May
4	four years	2008

How long have you taught French?
I have taught French for five years.
I have taught French since 2007.

C Ask and answer.   CD2 24

1. had a cat / May

I have studied English for six years.

2. studied English / six years

3. lived in New York / 2007

4. been at the hotel / yesterday evening

5. played soccer / one hour

Merci beaucoup.

6. taught French / six months

How long has she had a cat?
She has had a cat since May.

How long has he studied English?
He has studied English for six years.

D Listen and sing. CD2 25

How Long Has She Known Him?

How long has she known him?
How long has she known him?
How long has she known him?
  She's known him for a long, long time.
  She's known him since she was four.
  She met him in Singapore.
  They got married in a candy store.
  They had a baby in nineteen eighty-four.

They've been married
  for a long, long time.
They've been happy
  for a long, long time.
They've known each other
  for a long, long, long, long time.

Let's Learn More

A Learn the words. CD2 26

1. talking on the phone

2. visiting Bangkok

3. riding her bicycle

4. cleaning his room

5. waiting

6. playing baseball

B Make sentences. CD2 27

The children are busy. What are they doing? How long have they been doing it?

1 45 minutes

2 ten o'clock

3 early evening

4 2 hours

Jenny **is** riding her bicycle.
She **has been** riding her bicycle **for** 45 minutes.

Scott **is** waiting.
He **has been** waiting **since** ten o'clock.

C Ask and answer. CD2 28

1. last week

2. 15 minutes

3. one hour

4. noon

5. three o'clock

6. 30 minutes

How long **has** she **been** visiting Bangkok?
She **has been** visiting Bangkok **since** last week.

How long **has** she **been** waiting?
She **has been** waiting **for** 15 minutes.

D Listen and chant. CD2 29

How Long Have You Been Waiting?

How long have you been waiting for Ken?
I've been waiting for Ken since ten.

How long has he been talking to Sue?
He's been talking to Sue since two.

How long has Anne been taking a bath?
She's been taking a bath for an hour and a half.

How long have you been studying with Ray?
I started yesterday.

Let's Read

My Life with the Circus

My name is Mei. I'm an acrobat. Everyone in my family is an acrobat, too. We perform with a circus. I've been a performer since I was a little girl.

I don't go to school because we travel a lot. Teachers travel with us. Every morning, I study with other circus children. Every afternoon, I practice acrobatics with my family. I need strong arms and legs.

I jump, flip, and twirl in the air. My brother throws me, and my father catches me. It's hard work, but I like performing.

New Words

life
circus
acrobat / acrobatics
everyone
hard work

B **Choose the correct answer.** CD2 31

1. What does Mei do?
2. When does Mei practice?

☐ She's a student.
☐ every morning

☐ She's an acrobat.
☐ every afternoon

C Understand the vocabulary.

> We perform with a circus.

What does perform mean?

a.

b.

c.

D Ask your partner.

1. Have you ever been to a circus? How was it?
2. Have you ever seen acrobats? What did they do?

E Listen and write. Do you hear ar or ir? CD2 32

1. h_____d

2. tw_____l

3. _____m

4. g_____l

F Learn about words. Read and write.

> I like to perform.
> I am a performer.
> perform + er = performer

1. play + er = _____

2. paint + er = _____

3. _____ + _____ = teacher

4. _____ + _____ = farmer

Let's Review ✓

A Listen and check. (CD2 33)

1.  A ☐  B ☐

2.  A ☐  B ☐

3. A ☐ B ☐

4.  A ☐  B ☐

B Listen and check. (CD2 34)

1. A ☐ Portuguese is spoken in Brazil.
    B ☐ People in Brazil speak Portuguese.

2. A ☐ Spaghetti is eaten in Italy.
    B ☐ People in Italy eat spaghetti.

3. A ☐ People in France speak French.
    B ☐ French is spoken in France.

4. A ☐ Rice noodles are eaten in Vietnam.
    B ☐ People in Vietnam eat rice noodles.

C Listen and check. (CD2 35)

1. A ☐ He has been playing soccer for 45 minutes.
    B ☐ He has been playing soccer since yesterday.

2. A ☐ She has lived in Paris for two years.
    B ☐ She has been living in Paris since 2008.

3. A ☐ He has taught French since last spring.
    B ☐ He has been teaching French for six months.

4. A ☐ She has been waiting since 1:00 this afternoon.
    B ☐ She has waited for 15 minutes.

D Let's read about hieroglyphics.  (CD2 36)

Mystery Hunters

Matt and Megan's **Blog**

Writing with Pictures

In the ancient pyramids of Egypt, there were a lot of pictures on the walls. Scholars said the pictures were writing. These were called hieroglyphics. But no one was able to read them.

In 1799, French soldiers discovered a stone near Rosetta, a city in Egypt. This famous stone helped scholars read the pictures.

Today we don't use hieroglyphics, but we have rebus writing. A rebus is a picture puzzle. Each picture is a sound. When you read these sounds together, you will know the meaning.

Pyramid of Khafre, Egypt

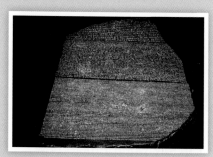

The Rosetta Stone in the British Museum

Hieroglyphics at Edfu Temple, Egypt

Try to read this.

👁 + ❤ + u
👁 = I
❤ = love
u = you

New Words

hieroglyphics
scholars
soldiers
stone
city
rebus

E Your turn!

Does your language use picture writing?

Try to make a rebus sentence.

Tell about your rebus.

Let's Talk

A **Listen and say.** (CD2 37)

Kate: Is that you?
Scott: Yes, it is.
Kate: Why were you hiding behind your dad?
Scott: I was shy.

Kate: Really? I don't believe it!
Scott: It's true. Sometimes I'm still shy.
Kate: Me, too. I'm shy when I meet new people.

Kate: How old were you in this photo?
Scott: I was five.
Kate: When did you learn how to do karate?
Scott: When I was four.
Kate: You looked cute!

(CD2 38)

> Really? I don't believe it!
> It's true.

B Practice the words. Ask and answer. CD2 39

1. outgoing

2. shy

3. friendly

4. studious

5. cheerful

6. generous

CD2 40

> What are they like?
> They are outgoing.

C Listen and sing. CD2 41

What's She Like?

What's she like?
  She's shy.
  She's very very shy.
Is she friendly?
  Yes, she is,
  but she's very very shy.
Is she studious?
  Yes, she is.

Is she cheerful?
  Yes, she is.
Is she generous?
  Yes, she is,
  but she's very very shy.

Let's Learn

A Learn the words.
CD2 42

1. learn how to walk

2. learn how to write my name

3. learn how to read

4. learn how to ride a bike

5. learn how to ice skate

6. learn how to tie my shoes

B Ask and answer.
CD2 43

Kate and Jenny are looking at old pictures.

age 5

age 1

age 4

age 6

When did you learn how to write your name?
I learned how to write my name when I was five.

C Ask and answer. CD2 44

1. one year old

2. six years old

3. eight years old

4. five years old

5. nine years old

6. four years old

When did he learn how to walk?
He learned how to walk **when** he **was** one.

one = one year old

D Listen and chant. CD2 45

How Old Were You?

How old were you when you
learned how to run?
  I was one, I was one.

How old were you when you
learned how to ski?
    I was three, I was three.

How old were you when you
went to the zoo?
  I was two, I was two.

I was three when I learned how to ski.
I was two when I went to the zoo.
I was one when I learned how to run.

Let's Learn More

A Learn the words. (CD2 46)

1. fly a helicopter

2. run a marathon

3. visit London

Hello! Bonjour! ¡Buenos días!

4. speak more languages

5. play golf

6. drive a car

7. act in a play

8. conduct an orchestra

B Make sentences. (CD2 47)

Scott, Jenny, Andy, and Kate are daydreaming.

I wish I could conduct an orchestra.

C Play a game. Ask and answer. CD2 48

> What does she wish she could do?
> She wishes she could speak more languages.

D What about you?

What do you wish you could do?

A Listen and read along. Then read again. (CD2 49)

Learn How to JUGGLE

Have you ever wished you could juggle?
Here's how. Start with three beanbags.

1 Throw beanbag A from hand to hand.
It's easy, but don't be careless. The
beanbag should come to eye level.

2 Use a pair of beanbags. Throw
beanbag A. Just before you catch it, throw
beanbag B.

3 Add one more beanbag. Throw
beanbag A. Just before you catch it,
throw beanbag B. Then, just before
you catch beanbag B, throw
beanbag C.

Practice a lot and you'll be a juggler!

New Words

juggle/juggler
eye level
careless
pair
add

B Choose the correct answer. (CD2 50)

1. How many beanbags should you start with? ☐ one beanbag   ☐ three beanbags
2. How should you throw beanbag A? ☐ carelessly   ☐ from hand to hand

C Understand the vocabulary.

> The beanbag should come to eye level.

What does eye level mean?

a.

b.

c.

D Ask your partner.

1. Have you ever seen a juggler?
2. Have you ever wished you could juggle?

E Listen and write. Do you hear air or er? (CD2 51)

1. p_____   2. juggl_____   3. flow_____   4. ch_____   5. h_____

F Learn about words. Read and write.

> Take care.
> Don't be careless.
>
> care + less = careless

1. color + less = _____   2. sugar + less = _____

3. _____ + _____ = toothless   4. _____ + _____ = harmless

Let's Talk

A Listen and say. (CD2 52)

Jenny: If you could go anywhere, where would you go?
Andy: I would go to Egypt.
Jenny: Why?
Andy: I'd like to see the pyramids.

Andy: What about you? Where would you go?
Jenny: I'd go to Antarctica.

Andy: Why would you go there? It's cold.
Jenny: I'd like to see penguins.
Andy: If you want to see penguins, we can go to the zoo.
Jenny: That's true. The zoo is warmer than Antarctica!

CD2 53

I would go to Egypt.
Why?
I'd like to see the pyramids.

I would = I'd

B Practice the words. Ask and answer. CD2 54

1. the Amazon jungle

2. Mt. Everest

3. the bottom of the ocean

4. the pyramids of Egypt

5. the moon

6. the equator

CD2 55

> If you could go anywhere, where would you go?
> I would go to the Amazon jungle.

C Listen and sing. CD2 56

If You Could Go Anywhere

If you could go anywhere,
Where would you go?
  I'd take a plane to Mexico.

If you could buy anything,
What would you buy?
  I'd buy an airplane and
learn how to fly.

If you could be anything,
What would you be?
  I'd be a tiger running up a tree.

If you could do anything,
What would you do?
  I'd have a party, and I'd invite you!

Let's Learn

A Learn the words. CD2 57

1. go to Antarctica

2. go to Mars

3. meet a TV star

4. meet a sports star

5. buy a pony

6. buy a motorbike

7. go kayaking

8. go skydiving

B Make sentences. CD2 58

The children are dreaming. What would they do if they could do anything?

If I could do anything, I would buy a pony.

C Ask and answer. (CD2 59)

1. go to Hawaii

2. meet a TV star

3. buy a bird

4. sail a boat

5. meet a sports star

6. go to New York

7. fly a helicopter

8. go rafting

> If you could do anything, what would you do?
> I would go to Hawaii.

D Listen and chant. (CD2 60)

If You Could Do Anything

If you could do anything,
what would you do?
  I'd climb Mt. Everest from Katmandu.
  I would, if I could. I would, if I could.

Konnichiwa!

If you could speak any language,
what would you speak?
  I'd speak French, English,
  Japanese, and Greek.
  I would, if I could. I would, if I could.

If you could buy anything,
  what would you buy?
    I'd buy a little plane and learn how to fly.
    I would, if I could. I would, if I could.

Let's Learn More

A Play a game.

Roll a die. Move your marker. Follow the directions at the top of page 71.

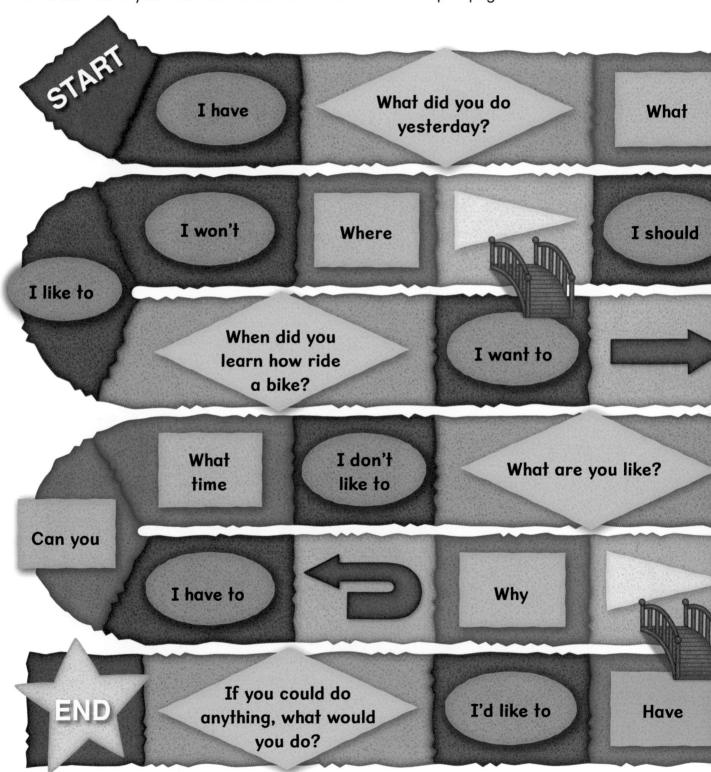

START

I have

What did you do yesterday?

What

I won't

Where

I should

I like to

When did you learn how ride a bike?

I want to

What time

I don't like to

What are you like?

Can you

I have to

Why

END

If you could do anything, what would you do?

I'd like to

Have

Directions

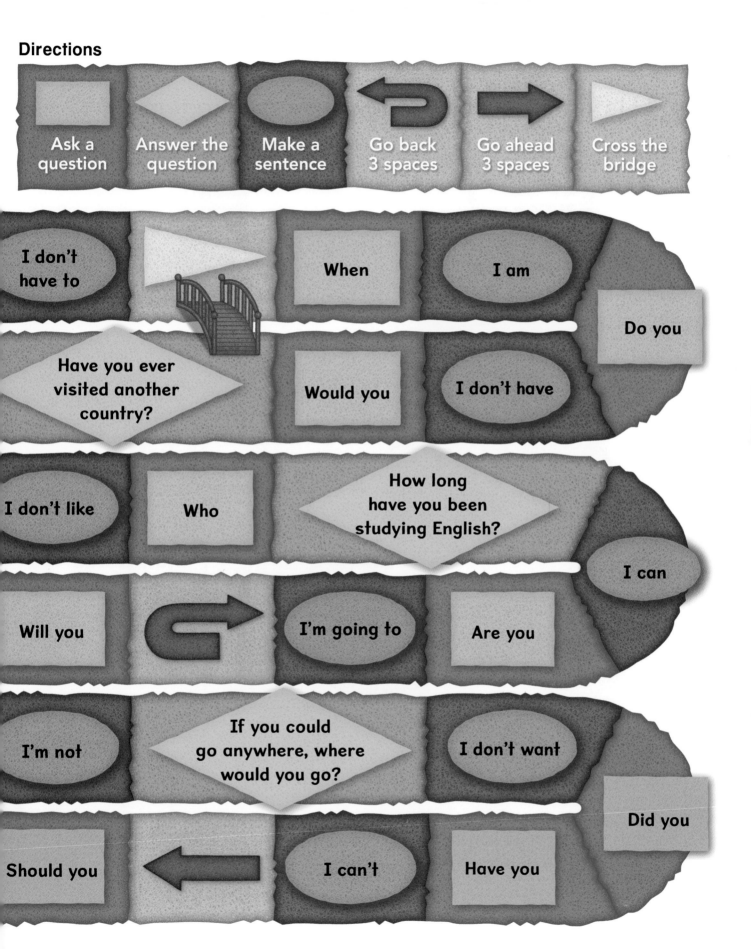

☐ Ask a question	◇ Answer the question
⬭ Make a sentence	↩ Go back 3 spaces
→ Go ahead 3 spaces	▷ Cross the bridge

I don't have to

When

I am

Do you

Have you ever visited another country?

Would you

I don't have

I don't like

Who

How long have you been studying English?

I can

Will you

I'm going to

Are you

I'm not

If you could go anywhere, where would you go?

I don't want

Did you

Should you

I can't

Have you

Let's Read

Koko

Koko is an amazing gorilla. She can talk. She learned how to use American Sign Language when she was one year old.

She was born on July 4th, 1971. Her full name is Hanabi-Ko. That means "fireworks child" in Japanese.

Every year, she has a birthday party. She and her friends eat her favorite foods—apples, carrots, corn, and tofu. There is always cake, too!

Koko likes kittens because their fur is soft. She likes to pet them and listen to them purr. If I could meet anyone, I would meet Koko!

New Words
American
Sign Language
corn
kittens
fur
pet
purr

B Choose the correct answer. (CD2 62)

1. What does Koko do every year? ☐ She pets kittens. ☐ She has a birthday party.
2. What animals does Koko like? ☐ kittens ☐ puppies

C Understand the vocabulary.

> She learned how to use American Sign Language when she was one year old.

What does American Sign Language mean?

a.

Hello!

b.

c.

Happy birthday, Koko

D Ask your partner.

1. Have you ever seen a gorilla? Where?
2. Have you ever seen someone use sign language?

E Listen and write. Do you hear or or ur? CD2 63

1. g_____illa   2. f_____   3. c_____n   4. p_____r

F Learn about words. Read and write.

> birthday = birth + day

1. beanbag = _____ + _____   2. football = _____ + _____

3. _____ = back + pack   4. _____ = pan + cake

Let's Review ✓

A Listen and check. (CD2 64)

1. He would go kayaking.
   ☐ True   ☐ False

2. He would meet a sports star.
   ☐ True   ☐ False

3. She would go to Mt. Everest.
   ☐ True   ☐ False

4. He would buy a motorbike.
   ☐ True   ☐ False

B Listen and check. (CD2 65)

1. **A** ☐ fly a helicopter
   B ☐ drive a car

2. **A** ☐ visit London
   B ☐ conduct an orchestra

3. **A** ☐ act in a play
   B ☐ speak more languages

4. **A** ☐ run a marathon
   B ☐ play golf

C Listen and match. (CD2 66)

1. Amy learned how to walk

a. when he was five.

2. Brad learned how to tie his shoes

b. when she was seven.

3. Nick learned how to ride a bike

c. when she was one.

4. Emma learned how to ice skate

d. when he was nine.

D Let's read about the mysterious drawings. (CD2 67)

Matt and Megan's **Blog**

The Condor

The Spider

Another view of the Nazca area

The Nazca Lines: Mysterious Drawings

In the Nazca desert in Peru, there are hundreds of giant drawings of animals and shapes. The drawings are thousands of years old and very large. Some are almost one kilometer long.

You can easily see the lines when you walk in the desert. But, on the ground, they just look like lines in the dirt. You can only see the pictures from high in the sky. And they were drawn long before there were airplanes.

Who made the Nazca drawings? How did they make them? And who looked at them from the sky?

It's a mystery.

New Words
desert
hundreds
thousands
one kilometer long

E Your turn!

Have you ever seen ancient drawings?

Who drew them?

What do you think? Write your opinion.

Where did you see them?

What do they mean?

Let's Go 6 Syllabus

Let's Remember

Look at this boat. It's colorful!

Which boy is faster?

Where's Andy? Have you seen him?

Have you ever eaten sushi?

What will you do after lunch?

Unit 1 School Days

Let's Talk	Let's Learn	Let's Learn More	Let's Read
Conversation: Whose scarf is that? It's Anna's scarf. Whose mittens are those? They're hers, too. Is that her glove, too? I think it's Jim's glove. Which boy is Jim? He's the boy over there. Jim, here's your other glove. Thanks for finding it. **Items:** scarf, mittens, gloves, glasses, belt, watch **Song:** Whose Boots Are These?	**School Activities:** watering the plants, feeding the fish, writing on the board, talking to the teacher, reading a textbook, writing an essay **Language:** Which boy is Scott? He's the boy who is watering the plants. Which girl is Lisa? **Chant:** Kim's Father Was Born in Seoul	**Activities:** talking on his cell phone, reading a magazine, walking in the park, drinking some water, playing a game, sitting on a bench **Language:** Jenny was sitting on a bench when it started to rain. What was he doing when it started to rain?	**Historical Story:** The First Ice Pop **Questions** **Vocabulary:** frozen **Phonics:** ow cow aw saw **Word Study:** mix + ed = mixed

Unit 2 At the Aquarium

Let's Talk	Let's Learn	Let's Learn More	Let's Read
Conversation: What a great day! It sure was! But I'm tired now. What did you like best? I think I liked the penguins best. They were cute. What about you? I liked the sharks. They were scary! **Adjectives:** amazed/amazing, bored/boring, interested/interesting, tired/tiring, excited/exciting, scared/scary **Chant:** The Racing Chant	**Places:** an aquarium, a tour, a lecture, an exhibit, a shark, an octopus **Language:** The shark was scary. The exhibit was amazing. She was amazed. **Chant:** Aquarium Chant	**Things to See and Do:** a jellyfish, a sea turtle, a squid, a video, a ride, a pedal boat **Language:** Kate said the sea turtles were amazing. He said he was amazed. She said the squid was scary.	**How-to Article:** Waves in a Bottle **Questions** **Vocabulary:** reuse **Phonics:** oi coin oo book **Word Study:** re + use = reuse

Let's Review Units 1 and 2 **Reading: Matt and Megan's Mystery Hunters Blog—Pyramids**

Unit 3 Going Shopping

Let's Talk	Let's Learn	Let's Learn More	Let's Read
Conversation: I need a present for my mother. What should I get her? Do you have any ideas? You could get her a teapot. Or you could get her a cookbook. She doesn't like tea, and she already has a lot of cookbooks. How about a scarf? That's a great idea! **Presents:** a scarf, a bracelet, a box of chocolates, a cookbook, a DVD, a book **Chant:** I Need a Present for My Mother	**Gifts:** a video camera, a necklace, a ring, a novel, a stuffed toy, earrings, golf clubs, a model **Language:** Should I get my sister a necklace or a ring? You should get her a ring. They should get him a novel. **Chant:** Today's My Brother's Birthday	**Activities:** bought a drink, made a bracelet, sent a picture, gave a present, showed a T-shirt, told a story **Language:** She showed him a T-shirt. What did she make her? She made her a bracelet.	**Story:** Happiness is a Clean Park **Questions** **Vocabulary:** since I was a baby **Phonics:** oo broom au August **Word Study:** kind + ness = kindness

Unit 4 Around Town

Let's Talk	Let's Learn	Let's Learn More	Let's Read
Conversation: Where's the food court? Let's look at the map. It's across from the music store. We should go this way. There's the food court. Where are the boys? They're over there, next to the ice cream shop. **Places:** ice cream shop, bakery, sports store, music store, clothing store, bookstore, food court, game store **Song:** Where's the Bookstore?	**Directions:** on the corner, around the corner from, on the right, on the left, across the street from, next to **Language:** Where's the ice cream shop? It's across the street from the bank. The bank is on the corner. It's next to the grocery store.	**Directions:** Go straight. Go to the corner. Turn left. Turn right. Go two blocks. Cross the street. **Language:** Go to the corner and turn right. Where are you? I'm at the bookstore. How do I get to the park? Go two blocks and turn right. **Chant:** I'm Looking for Joe	**Article:** The Blue Planet **Questions** **Vocabulary:** clockwise **Phonics:** ow blow or storm **Word Study:** rain + y = rainy

Let's Review Units 3 and 4 **Reading: Matt and Megan's Mystery Hunters Blog—Easter Island**

Unit 5 Explore the World

Let's Talk	Let's Learn	Let's Learn More	Let's Read
Conversation: Have you met Anh? No, I haven't. Where's she from? She's from Vietnam. Does Anh speak English? Yes, she does. She speaks Vietnamese and English, too. I'd like to meet her. Have you ever been on a homestay? **Countries and Nationalities:** Australia/Australian, Vietnam/Vietnamese, Thailand/Thai, Mexico/Mexican **Chant:** Homestay Plans	**Countries and Languages:** Brazil/Portuguese, France/French, Italy/Italian, Mexico/Spanish **Language:** People in France speak French. French is spoken in France. What language is spoken in Vietnam? **Song:** Have You Met Alice?	**International Foods:** black beans, croissants, spaghetti, rice noodles, burritos, meat pies **Language:** Where are black beans eaten? Black beans are eaten in Brazil. Croissants are eaten in France. Spanish is spoken in Mexico.	**Informational Story:** Chocolate **Questions** **Vocabulary:** discover **Phonics:** ea bread ou count **Word Study:** eat + ing = eating

Unit 6 Doing Things

Let's Talk	Let's Learn	Let's Learn More	Let's Read
Conversation: I'm sorry I'm late. That's OK. How long have you been waiting? A few minutes. Not long. Have you already bought your ticket? Yes, and I bought your ticket, too! I'm excited to see this movie! I've heard it's funny. I've heard it's scary. **Things done:** cleaned his desk, washed her hands, watched the movie, walked the dog, eaten dinner, fed the cat, gone to the store, done his homework **Chant:** Have You Finished Your Homework?	**Experiences:** studied English, lived in New York, taught French, played soccer, had a cat, been at the hotel **Language:** How long have you taught French? I've taught French for five years/since 2007. How long has she had a cat? **Song:** How Long Has She Known Him?	**Doing Things:** talking on the phone, visiting Bangkok, riding her bicycle, cleaning his room, waiting, playing baseball **Language:** Jenny is riding her bicycle. She has been riding her bicycle for 45 minutes/since ten o'clock. How long has she been visiting Bangkok? **Chant:** How Long Have You Been Waiting?	**Informational Story:** My Life with the Circus **Questions** **Vocabulary:** perform **Phonics:** ar hard ir twirl **Word Study:** perform + er = performer

Let's Review Units 5 and 6   **Reading: Matt and Megan's Mystery Hunters Blog—Hieroglyphics**

Unit 7 About Me

Let's Talk	Let's Learn	Let's Learn More	Let's Read
Conversation: Is that you? Yes, it is. Why were you hiding behind your dad? I was shy. Really? I don't believe it! It's true. I'm shy when I meet new people. How old were you in this photo? I was five. When did you learn how to do karate? When I was four. **Descriptions:** outgoing, shy, friendly, studious, cheerful, generous **Song:** What's She Like?	**Ages and Stages:** learn how to walk/write my name, learn how to read/ride a bike, learn how to ice skate/tie my shoes **Language:** When did you learn how to write your name? I learned how to write my name when I was five. **Chant:** How Old Were You?	**Wishes:** fly a helicopter, run a marathon, visit London, speak more languages, play golf, drive a car, act in a play, conduct an orchestra, **Language:** I wish I could conduct an orchestra. What does she wish she could do? She wishes she could speak more languages.	**How-to Article:** Learn How to Juggle **Questions** **Vocabulary:** eye level **Phonics:** air pair er juggler **Word Study:** care + less = careless

Unit 8 In the Future

Let's Talk	Let's Learn	Let's Learn More	Let's Read
Conversation: If you could go anywhere, where would you go? I would go to Egypt. Why? I'd like to see the pyramids. What about you? I'd go to Antarctica. I'd like to see penguins. **Places:** the Amazon jungle, Mt. Everest, the bottom of the ocean, the pyramids of Egypt, the moon, the equator **Song:** If You Could Go Anywhere	**In the Future:** go to Antarctica/Mars, meet a TV star/sports star, buy a pony/a motorbike, go kayaking/skydiving **Language:** If I could do anything, I would buy a pony. **Chant:** If You Could Do Anything	**Review Game**	**Article:** Koko **Questions** **Vocabulary:** American Sign Language **Phonics:** or gorilla ur fur **Word Study:** birthday = birth + day

Let's Review Units 7 and 8   **Reading: Matt and Megan's Mystery Hunters Blog—The Nazca Lines**

Word List